CW00327145

Successful
Assertiveness
in a week

Dena Michelli

Headway · Hodder & Stoughton

British Library Cataloguing in Publication Data

A catalogue for this title is available from the
British Library

ISBN 0 340 60893 5

First published 1994
Impression number   10   9   8   7   6   5   4   3   2   1
Year   1999   1998   1997   1996   1995   1994

Typeset by Multiplex Techniques Ltd, St Mary Cray, Kent.
Printed for Hodder & Stoughton Educational, a division of
Hodder Headline Plc, 338 Euston Road, London NW1 3BH
by Colorcraft Ltd, Hong Kong

the *Institute*
of *Management*

F O U N D A T I O N

The Institute of Management (IM) is at the forefront of management development and best management practice. The Institute embraces all levels of management from students to chief executives. It provides a unique portfolio of services for all managers, enabling them to develop skills and achieve management excellence.

For information on the benefits of membership, please contact:

Department HS
Institute of Management
Cottingham Road
Corby
Northants NN17 1TT

Tel 0536 204222
Fax 0536 201651

This series is commissioned by the Institute of Management Foundation.

C O N T E N T S

Taking the decision to adopt *assertive* behaviour will mark the beginning of a new way of life: a way of life where you make your own decisions and choices without feeling guilty, and where *you* are in control, not those around you.

By working through some simple steps, and by testing the techniques out in a 'safe' environment, you will soon become confident in your new-found powers of assertion. You will be able to command the respect of others, achieve your personal and professional goals *and* be popular – if you choose.

The steps to assertive behaviour are:

- Understand the different styles of communication and the effect they have
- Identify your own style(s) of communication
- Know your own worth *and* the worth of others
- Be clear about your goals
- Be prepared to learn from your success *and* failures
- Be flexible, and don't expect too much
- Learn to listen

Preparing the foundations

Today, we will prepare the foundations for developing assertive behaviour and learn the different styles of communication: *passive, passive/aggressive, aggressive* and *assertive.*

There are two main tasks here. First, identify your own

style of communication:

- Passive
- Passive/Aggressive
- Aggressive
- Assertive

Second, know your worth:

- Understand yourself
- Accept and forgive yourself for the way you are
- Decide to change – *if you want to*
- Give yourself permission to succeed – *and fail*

Identify your style of communication

In order to understand ourselves, and why we don't behave assertively, we must first examine our current *patterns of behaviour*. We will not dwell on our failures; we will merely use them for information, and for our motivation to change.

Note your behavioural pattern, in both your personal and professional lives. It is this that determines the way people respond to you and it is this in turn that determines the outcome of all your communication.

If you have difficulty identifying the pattern in yourself, ask a friend to help – but remember, they are doing you a favour.

For instance: are you very aggressive, uncompromising, fixed in your views, intolerant or impatient? Are you sarcastic, manipulative, dismissive, arrogant or superior? Are you acquiescent, apologetic, deferring, self-effacing or inferior?

It is interesting to note that most people who want to develop assertive behaviour fit into the last category – that of 'victim'.

People always treat you the way you 'ask' to be treated. Understanding what you are 'asking for' is half the battle. You are now in a position to observe yourself carefully, and honestly, and make the changes that *will* make the changes.

Don't feel hopeless at this point; from now on, everything is a positive step.

Remember, all it takes to change is a decision.

Most people's behaviour patterns will demonstrate some characteristics from each of the four categories noted above – *passive, passive/aggressive, aggressive* and *assertive* – depending on the circumstances of the communication. However, one category will most likely dominate your style. Read through the descriptions below and see which one holds true for you most of the time.

Passive
Passive behaviour is usually associated with the 'loser': one who is always backing down, giving in and being submissive. Apologies are rife in this mode of communication, as are reluctant agreements and negative statements about the self. Passive behaviour conveys the message 'you're OK, I'm not OK.'

Passive/aggressive
Passive/aggressive behaviour is usually associated with the 'saboteur'. It is by no means overt, but the aggressive motivation is obvious nonetheless. The distinguishing features of this mode of communication are sarcastic comments, comments with double meanings and non-verbal signals such as mockingly gazing heavenwards. The underlying message is 'I'm not OK, you're not OK.'

Aggressive

Aggressive behaviour takes no account of the rights of others. Although this person may be perceived to be a 'go-getter' or one of life's 'winners', they are usually feared and their style encourages deceitful behaviour from others who would rather not face up to the aggressor's wrath. The message conveyed by this person is 'I'm OK, you're not OK.'

Assertive

Assertive communication does not diminish or 'put down' another human being, it does not trespass on any human rights and it does not shy away from important issues. Rather, it encourages satisfactory communication where everyone's needs are met in the best way. The identifying characteristic of assertive behaviour is the use of 'I' statements. This indicates that the person communicating is taking responsibility for the message that is being conveyed. For example, 'I am not happy with this decision, I would like to discuss it further.' This form of communication is based on respect for self and others. It is driven by the belief that 'I'm OK, you're OK.' There are no losers.

A word of caution. Assertive behaviour does not necessarily mean that you get your way all the time. It *does* mean that the chances of getting to the best solution, with everyone's self-esteem intact, are significantly enhanced.

The main characteristic associated with each style of communication is shown overleaf. If you have difficulty determining whether you are passive, passive/aggressive, assertive or aggressive, you may be able to identify with one of these characteristics instead. You can then find your dominant style by reading the definition below.

Surrendering	Undermining	Facilitating	Argumentative
☐	☐	☐	☐
Passive	Passive/ aggressive	Assertive	Aggressive

This should give you an idea of where the work on your communication skills should begin.

If you fall naturally into the passive category, you will most probably be very keen to change your behaviour to the more assertive type. You will recognise that the adoption of this style of communication will mean that you can, at last, stop undermining and diminishing yourself. It holds many rewards for you.

If however, you fall into the aggressive category, it will be hard for you to move into assertive behaviour because it will feel as if you are losing control. Be brave; you are actually *gaining* control and winning commitment from those communicating with you.

For those of you who are passive/aggressive, at the moment you are actually letting *others* determine how you feel. You probably expect them to guess your feelings, feel sorry for causing them and change their behaviour towards you. It would be far less stressful to start taking control and start making your own choices.

If you are still unsure of your dominant style of communicating behaviour, work through the simple questionnaire overleaf. Do not worry if your responses fall into all the different categories; identify with the strongest trend. The mix of responses will help you focus on the specific areas in your style that you may wish to change.

It really doesn't matter how you label yourself as long as you know what your objectives are.

Broadly speaking, if most of your responses fall into the 'Sometimes' category, you tend to be aggressive or passive/ aggressive. If they fall into the 'Never' category you are certainly passive. If you find that your responses are predominantly in the 'Often' column, you are well on the way to being assertive.

Know your worth

Understand yourself
We all have basic human rights:

Communication Style Questionnaire

		Sometimes	Often	Never
1	I feel that I represent myself well in all communications	☐	☐	☐
2	My ideas are considered valuable and often adopted	☐	☐	☐
3	My opinions are sought by others	☐	☐	☐
4	I am able to make complaints and am satisfied with the outcome	☐	☐	☐
5	I am able to criticise another without causing offence	☐	☐	☐
6	I can communicate effectively in a group	☐	☐	☐
7	I am able to ask for help	☐	☐	☐
8	I use manipulative techniques for getting my own way	☐	☐	☐
9	I find I lose my temper	☐	☐	☐
10	People find that I am good at talking through ideas and problems	☐	☐	☐
11	I am free from disabling stress	☐	☐	☐
12	I feel comfortable with who I am	☐	☐	☐

- The right to choose
- The right to 'be'
- The right to be respected
- The right to make mistakes
- The right to say 'no'
- The right to ask for what we want
- The right to ask for what we need

It is *always* our fears that block us from developing assertive behaviour. What are yours?

'I will lose my friends', 'I will make a fool of myself', 'No one will like me any more', 'I will become irritating', ...' (fill in your own).

Our fears are *always* larger than reality. Face them; they have a wonderful habit of shrinking.

Accept and forgive yourself for the way you are
It is very easy to put yourself down. We are our own worst critics.

It is helpful to know that we are:

- *what* we are supposed to be
- *where* we are supposed to be
- *doing what* we are supposed to do

Release all your disappointments and guilts – forgive yourself. Everything that you have done and experienced has brought you to this point of change. *Everything is to play for*.

Decide to change – if you want to

In making your decision to change your behaviour, you may find it helpful to project forward in time and imagine how it would look, and feel, if you were in control of your communication. Compare this to how you feel now.

The power of 'imaging' or 'visualising' cannot be over-stressed. It is a very useful tool for achieving your objectives, whatever they are.

By 'bringing to mind' or 'picturing in your mind's eye' your desired state, you are actually putting images into your subconscious mind that ultimately determine your behaviour. Your subconscious mind can only work in images, it does not understand timescales or conditions. Imagine yourself as you would like to 'be' and your subconscious will work tirelessly to make this a reality. It cannot fail. Keep reinforcing the images time after time, using positive affirmations if this helps (see Monday for more on this) and the old patterns will soon be obliterated and replaced with the new ones that you have chosen.

Old habits die hard, but they do die with persistence and determination.

If you continue to behave as you have always behaved, people will continue to treat you as they have always treated you.

Give yourself permission to succeed – and fail
You are embarking on a journey of transformation. It will not always be easy but it will be rewarding.

There will be times when you can't put a foot wrong. Your communication with others will be assertive and effective and you will be amazed at how differently you are perceived. There will also be times when you slip back into your old habits.

All this is part of your learning. Don't beat yourself up when you fail. You will be grateful for all these experiences sometime in the future when it really matters.

By now you should have identified your dominant style of communication and decided whether or not you are completely happy to continue in this vein.

If you decide to make changes in the way you communicate and in the way you are perceived by your colleagues, then proceed with enthusiasm; there is much you can gain from the following chapters.

Summary

To recap, the different communication styles are broadly divided into the following categories:

- Passive
- Passive/Aggressive
- Assertive
- Aggressive

These are loosely associated with the following characteristics:

- Victim
- Manipulator
- Achiever
- Dictator

Creating winning scenarios

Today will bring us that little bit closer to being in control of our own lives – asserting ourselves in the way we choose. We will look at:

- 'Winning' language
- Positive affirmations
- Creative visualisation
- Building self-esteem

Those who are adept at turning on assertive behaviour are also quite able to observe their actions, talk themselves through their learning and test the effect of new behaviours. Self-knowledge is the key to taking control of our lives.

Observing, questioning and asking for feedback is vital if we are to succeed.

'Winning' language

'Winning' language is the language of assertive behaviour. It speaks more than words to those you communicate with and tells them that you are in control.

Those who recognise this quality in you will nonetheless be hard pressed to say exactly what it is that you are doing to give them this impression. Actually, it is a subtle combination of body language, mental attitude and verbal language.

Remember, *it's not what you say that counts, it's the way that you say it*.

The 'winning' qualities of an assertive communicator are:

- Direct, clear language
- An ability to demonstrate understanding and to empathise ('active listening skills')
- An ability to build rapport and maintain relationships
- Good posture, voice and eye contact
- Confidence in what you say – no self-effacing comments or profuse apologies!

Let's look at these qualities in more detail.

Direct clear language

Language can be a very inadequate and clumsy tool for communication. It can also be beautifully simple and, combined with reinforcing messages through the various physical channels of communication (body language), can be extremely effective and evocative.

Here are some simple rules to help you practise assertive, 'winning', language:

- *Set the scene* by describing – very briefly – what you are referring to: 'When you called a meeting last Friday, I . . .'
- *Simplicity, clarity and brevity* are key to assertive communication. Do not ramble; you will lose the attention of your audience. Make your point quickly.
- *Take responsibility* for what you are saying. This is done by using 'I' statements. Here are two examples of 'I' statements; one negative and one positive: 'I am unhappy about the way this project is proceeding.' 'I'm delighted with the outcome of this meeting.'
- *Use repetition* if you feel that your message isn't getting across, but restructure your statement the second time.
- *Use silence appropriately* – it can say more than words. Don't be afraid of it; try it out.

Active listening skills

Active listening ranks highly in the league table of the various communication skills. It enables you to empathise with your audience and build successful relationships.

Good listeners do several things when communicating. They:

- *Paraphrase* – briefly summarise what has just been said
- *Ask 'open' questions* to elicit good information – 'how' and 'what' ('why' can sound whiney or inquisitorial)
- *Show an interest* – maintain good eye contact and prompt more communication by nodding from time to time, using encouraging words like 'Yes', 'Ah ha' and 'Mmm'
- *Give feedback* – reflect back what they believe is being said

Building rapport and maintaining relationships

Everybody needs to feel liked and valued, and they will be generous in their dealings with you if you manage to develop a healthy rapport. It is a good investment *if done genuinely and generously*. If you do this as a manipulative technique, your motivation will almost certainly be exposed.

Developing true rapport is based on taking an interest in the other party, understanding and remembering what they have said and remembering to acknowledge significant events or achievements.

Body language also plays a part in developing rapport (more of this on Friday).

It sometimes helps to write down others' activities as well as your own if you are forgetful. However, you will soon learn that if you manage to develop active listening skills and build empathetic relationships, you will start to remember things more reliably. This is because you will have been concentrating on what the other person has been saying, and you will have heard yourself summarise the main points.

Hearing yourself say something really does help you to remember. *Talking to yourself is not a sign of madness; it is a valuable aide memoire.*

Good posture, voice and eye contact
It is somewhat galling to note that only about 7 per cent of what you say (the words you use) contributes towards the message you are trying to convey.

Much more of the message – 38 per cent – is carried in your voice. This includes tone, pitch, speed and the quality of your voice.

The remainder, some 55 per cent, is conveyed by your body. This, of course, is why the telephone can be so misleading. Messages have a tendency to become distorted when confined to only two of the three channels of communication available to you (words and voice, with no visible channel).

A large proportion of the messages you convey with your body are carried in the face, and more specifically, the eyes.

Good posture and an upright walk looks good and conveys confidence. Slouching or shuffling along gives completely the opposite impression. Try walking towards yourself in front of a mirror or catch a glimpse of yourself in a shop window. Notice the difference when you actively try to improve the way you move.

Assertive body language will be covered more fully in Friday's lesson. But there are several simple rules to consider for the time being:

- *Stand or sit proud* – taking up as little space as possible conveys lack of confidence or weakness
- *Gesture appropriately* – gestures can help in the understanding of a message when used sensibly. Try not to overdo it, however; a lot of extravagant gesturing can be very distracting.
- *Don't fidget* – this will make you appear nervous, as no doubt you are, if you are fidgeting.

The use and quality of your *voice* and the way sound resonates around the bone structure of your face will contribute to the other person's perception of what you are saying.

A high-pitched, whiney voice, for example, which for some of us is our natural style, conveys a 'victim' message: 'I'm really rather weak and pathetic and I'm throwing myself on your mercy!' (Note how assertively this message is being conveyed – lots of 'I' statements!) This style of voice can also sound spoilt and petulant.

By contrast, a loud, deep voice delivering words like machine gun fire sounds incredibly aggressive.

Notice your own dominant style. Would you like to change it?

The optimum style – if there really is such a thing – is a calm pace, pitched mid-range with good intonation and clearly enunciated words. It's not always appropriate, of course, but it does for most eventualities.

To communicate assertively, you must maintain good *eye contact*. Aim to maintain almost consistent eye contact while you are listening to another person. It is not so easy, indeed it can be actively disconcerting, to maintain constant eye contact while you are talking. Your eyes will help in the expression of your message and will no doubt be on the move much of the time. However, return your glance regularly to your subject throughout your talk; it will help you pick up how the other person is feeling about what you are saying.

It is worth noting that if your body is out of synchronisation with your words, your hidden agenda will immediately be revealed – if not precisely what it is, at least the fact that you have one!

Confidence in what you say
Confidence is fine if you have it, but most unassertive people are sadly lacking in this department. However, here are some useful tips that you can learn to incorporate in your repertoire very easily.

- *Say what you mean and mean what you say* – be succinct and use the 'I' statement.
- *Never apologise* – unless you sincerely mean it, then only do it once
  (Notice how politicians and business leaders almost *never* apologise. Are we really convinced that they *never* make mistakes?)
- *Don't claim to be a fool* to compensate for feeling a fool. We often do this to prompt a contradiction. One of the dangers of this strategy is that you will be believed.

Positive affirmations

Used in the right way, positive affirmations can be enormously helpful. They retrain the brain to think about ourselves differently.

If we have a poor self-opinion (usually as a result of a series of childhood experiences), then as soon as we suffer a loss of confidence, we will return to this level of negativity. It will take repeated effort to overcome this tendency and to replace it with something more positive.

For some people, positive affirmations can be very helpful in this process.

Positive affirmations are constant repetitions of a belief we wish to install in our brains to replace the less healthy beliefs we have grown up with.

And they will have to be constantly repeated: if you think how long you have lived with your own negativity, just think how often you will have to repeat a desired belief before it will outweigh, and triumph over, the negative belief that is so firmly lodged in your brain.

Every time we have a thought, an electrical impulse sets off along a particular route through the brain. After this same thought has been thought many times, a physical path becomes etched in the brain. This will deepen with every thinking of the thought. If this happens to be a negative or undermining thought, it will colour what you project to others. A new path must be created, therefore, that is even deeper, and therefore easier, for the thought to follow – the path of least resistance. This can be achieved through positive affirmations.

Say your positive affirmations every day, like a mantra, and eventually you will find that you have reprogrammed your brain and installed a healthier belief.

There are several rules for designing positive affirmations.

- They must be in the present – 'I am . . . '
- They must *not* be conditional – 'When I . . . then I will . . . '
- They must *not* be undermined – hidden message: 'Who am I trying to fool with all this stuff anyway?!'
- They must be about *you*; nobody else.
- They must be spoken out loud – in private if you wish, but it is important to *hear* yourself say them.

Examples of good affirmations are:

- 'I can handle it'
- 'I am professionally competent'
- 'I am a valuable and capable member of the team'

Creative visualisation

Creative visualisation is an extremely powerful technique for 'seeing' and 'fixing' your far-distant goals in your mind's eye and for planning and rehearsing the execution of the tasks that lead to the achievement of your goals.

The subconscious mind works in images, and when these are clear, it will work tirelessly to turn these images into reality.

What you need for effective creative visualisation is a starting point, and an end point. That is to say, you need to understand your current situation completely and notice how far away you are from reaching your goal.

This is not a negative exercise, it is an unemotional and non-judgemental appraisal, to enable you to take realistic and positive action.

Once you have isolated and fully understood your current situation, you must then form a very clear image of your goal and 'see', 'feel' and 'sense' it in your mind. Imagine it from a detached point of view, as if you were watching a film, and imagine it as if you were actually there, participating in it or living with it. Imagine it every way you can until you have a precise picture. Do not dismantle that picture; hold it clearly in your mind. Return to it regularly so that it becomes reinforced, time and again.

Set some time aside for this visualisation so that you can build its strength over time. Do not try to hurry the achievement of your goal. Your subconscious will take the strain between your current situation and your desired state and will work to transform the first image into the second.

This method of achieving what you desire is infallible when done diligently. Indeed, you will probably have some personal experience of a time when you did this instinctively when you desired something so badly, and so clearly, that you managed to bring it to reality.

Try it with big desires and small, but make sure that they are yours and not anyone else's. You will not be able to use it to manipulate others to do what you want!

In summary, here are the basic steps to effective creative visualisation – a method that all successfully assertive people adopt without even thinking about it.

- Develop a clear image of your goal
- Breathe it, feel it, smell it, examine it from all angles
- Notice your current situation and your distance from the goal
- Plan and execute your first and second steps only
- Do something else and leave your subconscious to work on the next stage undisturbed. Do not interfere, and do not undermine your images
- The next steps will come to you in their own time
- Return to reinforce the image of your goal and your current position regularly but infrequently
- Trust the process, it will work

Planning and rehearsing the tasks that have to be performed before reaching your goal are like 'mini' creative visualisations. Each step can be treated in the same way as those listed above for a major goal. Never plan more than two steps ahead, however, as the path your subconscious mind leads you down may be different from the one you expect. Follow it: it will probably be more creative and more effective.

If you have no clear idea of the tasks, don't worry; they will pop into your mind when the moment is right.

When you have executed the tasks in your mind's eye, you will find that the ease with which you perform them in reality will be truly remarkable.

Once you have a clear idea of your goal, everything you do and every decision you make will be in the context of this goal.

Building self-esteem

Self-esteem, as opposed to ego, is very difficult to recapture once it is lost. Self-esteem is a measure of how you value yourself, and it is built up from your first breath – or, as in many cases, it is destroyed by damaging relationships. It is one of the most helpful personal qualities that you can possess, because from it stems the belief that you are worthy to succeed.

Sometimes people try to camouflage their low self-esteem by portraying excessive confidence. This is just 'noise' used to mask their heart-felt feelings of vulnerability and inadequacy. Don't be fooled or intimidated by this. Recognise it as a human solution to intolerable emotional discomfort. In this way, the threat of what appear to be very confident people will disappear and you will be able to meet them on an equal footing.

Using some of the techniques described above can help to build self-esteem and confidence, but there is no substitute for knowing yourself and knowing the areas in which you are most likely to excel. There is nothing so powerful as a series of successes to lead you towards the establishment of a healthy self-esteem, so plan for them.

Here are some thoughts for you to consider when trying to raise the level of your self-esteem:

- Let go of being responsible for those around you: take responsibility for your own choices and feelings
- Don't take yourself too seriously – once you lose your sense of humour, you have lost control
- Have realistic expectations of yourself: do not compare yourself to an ideal – you will always fall short
- Let go of your 'mad' self-perceptions – in your rational mind you will know what these are
- Know yourself; understand what is blocking your progress – usually fear of failure, or guilt that you are not good enough
- Nurture yourself – give yourself treats

Summary

Today you were offered some techniques that will enable you to be successfully assertive and to be seen to be in charge of your own actions. Don't diminish the importance of these tools. If you practise them often they will become second nature to you.

Soon your colleagues will notice that you are more decisive, effective and confident. This is excellent news for those who are managing or leading a team.

Remember therefore:

Project a positive image by:

- Adopting 'winning language'
- Using body language to reinforce your messages
- Developing a positive mental attitude
- Listening actively
- Building rapport through empathy

All this will lead to:

- A healthy self-esteem

Please note, there is no danger of training your personality out of yourself. Your personal style will continue to distinguish you among your colleagues – even if they too are successful at being assertive. Indeed, you will feel freer to express yourself individually as you become more comfortable with your powers of assertion. If you find that you are radically eccentric, still don't worry: the British have a great capacity for embracing this quality!

Dealing with the negative

Today will help you negotiate your way through the most
difficult territory in communication terms – that of the
'negative':

- Handling anger – yours and others'
- Resolving conflict
- Giving and receiving criticism
- Saying 'No'
- Handling rejection and failure

Handling anger – yours and others'

Most of us nurse an innate fear of anger. This may be a
throwback to our childhood years when we felt powerless

and vulnerable. When we encounter 'anger', therefore, our bodies tend to react by preparing us for 'fight or flight' – rapid heartbeat, rapid breathing, an increased supply of blood to the muscles – all as a result of the release of adrenalin into the blood stream. This is the natural defence mechanism that 'kicks in' when we are threatened, and, at the right time, it is a life-saver.

In most modern situations, however, this reaction is both inappropriate and unhelpful and we must learn to override this natural tendency by reducing our fear. This may be achieved by understanding anger.

Anger is just energy. It will be directed by an angry person indiscriminately at things or specifically at you. It is like a heat-seeking missile looking for a target and it merely needs to be deflected or damped.

The thing to remember about anger is that it is not *you*, the personality, that has precipitated the anger, but some action or stance that you have taken which has struck an unhappy chord with the other. *You* are still an acceptable human being with rights. The anger you are fielding has always arisen as a result of the other person's conditioning – sometimes unreasonable conditioning. The same is true of your own anger, of course.

The best method for dealing with another's anger – in all but the pathological cases – is first to remove your personal investment in the situation. View it dispassionately from a distance and observe its nature while letting it burn itself out. Don't fuel it.

Try to identify the source of the anger by listening carefully to what is being said – or SHOUTED. You may find that the angry person feels criticised, unimportant, thwarted, hurt – any number of emotions. This will give you a clue as to how to proceed.

If you are still struggling, ask questions to clarify your understanding but try not to be patronising or unctuous.

If you are in a public place and you feel embarrassed, just remember that you are the one in control at the moment and that it is the other party that is drawing attention to themselves – and they will, of course; we are a sensation-seeking society.

Once the heat has died down, communicate your understanding of the situation from the other's point of view and negotiate a way forward or a resolution.

If you feel that it is important to douse the anger rapidly, a useful technique to adopt is to match the energy being expended. This is done by making a loud proclamation such as 'I UNDERSTAND WHY YOU ARE SO UPSET and I would feel exactly the same if I were you, but . . .' As you proceed, you can drop the pitch of your voice and start to take control.

As an observer, you can often hear when the heat is rising in a situation because voices tend to increase in pitch. Voices become high and whiney and words are delivered like machine-gun fire. This is counter to all hope of control.

Try not to be tempted to use 'reason'. The purpose of reasoning is to get the other to agree that their behaviour is unreasonable, and nobody wants to do that when they are at fever pitch. This will obviously build resentment. Reasoning can be a passive/aggressive stance as it attempts to lure the other into a submissive position.

Remember – you always have the option to walk away.

When you feel angry yourself, try the distancing technique. (Deep breathing or counting to 10 helps some people.) You can observe your own behaviour quite dispassionately with practice. The observations you make of yourself will contribute enormously to your self-knowledge if you can do it honestly. You will reap untold rewards in your ability to communicate assertively.

Here is a checklist for helping you to cope with anger:

- Distance yourself; don't take anger personally
- Understand the cause of the anger by listening and observing carefully
- Say nothing until the anger has died down
- Use a low-pitched voice and speak clearly
- Respect yourself and the other party; you still both have rights
- Once a certain degree of tranquillity has been achieved, demonstrate understanding by acknowledging the other's viewpoint – not the same thing as agreeing with it (don't use reason)
- Negotiate a way forward
- If all else fails, walk away. This is another way of respecting yourself

Resolving conflict

For the purposes of clarity, conflict is treated as a separate entity from anger, although one can sometimes lead to the other.

Conflict can be invisible, insidious and elusive, particularly with those of the passive/aggressive persuasion. It can lead to an impasse, a block which is extremely difficult to move. We have seen many such conflicts in the industrial quarter with unresolved disputes leading to the destruction of an organisation.

Conflict can also be clear, reasonable and helpful. Used positively, it can sharpen the mind, increase understanding and lead towards a very satisfying and creative solution.

Many of the techniques for dealing with conflict are similar to those used for dealing with anger. The issues may be more complex because the two opposing positions are often well thought out and rehearsed in advance. The goals of the two parties may at first appear totally different and incompatible. This is rarely the case in reality, however.

Here is a checklist for resolving conflict:

- Establish the desired outcome and priorities for both parties
- Acknowledge and appreciate the other's position
- Discuss the points of mutual agreement to establish rapport

- Compromise on issues that are not central to the desired outcome
- Identify and clarify those points that are left unresolved
- Delve for deeper understanding by questioning thoroughly and listening carefully
- Negotiate a resolution or agree a plan for the next step

Giving and receiving criticism

This is always difficult territory. We usually give criticism badly because we are not very good at receiving it.

Giving criticism
Giving early critical feedback prevents a bad situation developing into dreadful one.

Here is a guide to giving criticism which may be helpful:

- Be considerate and, above all, be private
- Don't 'pussyfoot' around, have confidence in what you want to say (use 'I' statements)
- Take responsibility for the criticism; don't do it because you have been cajoled into doing so, and don't base it on rumour
- Make sure the criticism is based on the behaviour you would like to see changed, not on the personality of the individual being criticised
- Use positive body language (see Friday)

Constructive criticism is often referred to as 'feedback' and may be given on the back of what is called a 'positive stoke'. For instance: 'I liked the way you handled that call but it might portray better customer service if you used their name.'

Receiving criticism
None of us enjoys being criticised. Indeed, most of us are looking for a confirmation that we are liked and accepted the way we are. However, if we put our vulnerabilities behind us for a moment, it really can be very helpful to hear how others perceive our behaviour or our work. We are then in a better position to make the desired adjustments – if we feel that they are valid.

Sometimes we may feel that the criticism is unfair. If this is the case, try to retain every vestige of dignity possible, state your disagreement and move on. Try not to argue for yourself; you will not convince anybody and you will hand your power straight to the person doing the criticising.

Here is a quick checklist for receiving criticism:

- Attend carefully to what is being said
- Judge for yourself if it is valid; if not, disregard it and move on
- Do not argue; you will only draw attention to your vulnerabilities

If you are unfortunate enough to be criticised in public, a dignified reaction will elicit a disproportionate amount of respect from observers while the standing of the person doing the criticising will be severely diminished.

Saying 'No'

We are rewarded with masses of praise when we acquiesce. This is not surprising as, in doing so, we have taken responsibility for somebody else's task or burden. By comparison, the emotional reward for saying 'No' is somewhat barren.

We are often made to feel guilty and mean – criticised even. This is a form of manipulation, a last-ditch attempt to make you change your mind and cooperate after all.

Dealing with this requires a particular kind of resilience. It helps if you really do believe that it is perfectly acceptable to make choices according to your own set of priorities, values and beliefs. This does not mean to say that you need always say 'No', just to prove that you are in control of your own decisions. What it does mean is that you *can* say 'No'.

Here is a list of useful tips that you can use when wishing to say 'No':

- Really mean it – if you don't it will probably show and the person making the request will probe and prise until you change your mind
- If you want to think about your response, say 'I will get back to you' or 'I need some time to think about this.' This is your right – who is doing who the favour?
- Don't milk the apology, wring your hands anxiously or overplay the excuses
- You may be able to offer a compromise solution

Handling rejection and failure

It is very difficult to separate rejection and failure because they are so intrinsically linked together.

They can bring utter despair and dejection, a feeling of foolishness, of being unworthy and so many other negative emotions.

Accepting that this is the case for so many of us, the healthy thing to do is to learn from these emotions, work with them and view them from a more positive perspective. This may sound trite and unhelpful, but with a bit of determination your perceived failures and consequent feelings of rejection will disappear into humorous anecdotes.

'Did I tell you about the time when I asked the Chairman if he was authorised to be in the building?'

Try not to confuse your true self-worth with one fleeting, albeit negative, experience. To be too harsh on yourself is unhelpful and at a time like this, you need all the forgiveness and understanding you can get – even if it has to come from you.

One useful tactic you may like to employ to avoid the feeling of total defeat is to make a series of contingency plans. In thinking through possible, probable or even improbable scenarios that are likely to tarnish your reputation, you can spend some useful time preparing coping strategies. In this way, you can redeem yourself rapidly and divert the destructive feelings of rejection and failure into a more positive arena.

Don't dwell for too long on the negative, however; you may find you have creatively visualised something you would rather not come true.

These may be helpful as part of your survival package

- Try not to link your own worth to the negative experience
- Never be bereft of alternatives – develop contingency plans
- Be kind to yourself
- Know that the significance of negative experiences changes with time
- Try to distil some learning from the experience – it will protect you next time

The whole gamut of negative experiences and emotions are uncomfortable at best. But having conquered your fear and having successfully dealt with a few difficult situations, you will soon re-educate your reflex reactions to cooperate with the way you would rather be.

Developing a balanced view on these matters will make you much stronger because you won't be trying to avoid issues; instead you will be making choices and following them through confidently.

A word of caution. You are not invincible, so try not to get over-zealous in your enthusiasm to tackle negativity. There definitely are situations that are best avoided because there can be no victor in their resolution. Anger that turns to physical violence is an irrational act and therefore cannot be approached in a rational way. In these circumstances, self-preservation is the key and if your body prepares you for flight – do it!

Summary

In summary, what we have been dealing with today is 'negative energy'. When this is understood, fear can evaporate, and this energy can be transformed into a positive outcome. Positive for everyone.

Being able to identify with another human being caught in the grip of fury may enable us to empathise with their plight, and in so doing enable us to behave generously.

It is worth noting that behaving assertively, as you would be if you managed to control an angry exchange without destruction to either party's ego, is not always what you wish to achieve. Sometimes you may choose a good fight; so SHOUT BACK IF YOU WANT TO SHOUT BACK, but be sure you are doing this because you really want this pleasure and be sure to enjoy every moment of it. This is honouring yourself. But you may have to be prepared to pick up the pieces of your relationship later.

Alternatively, walk away if you want to walk away.

Creating a positive impression in the private arena

There are many possibilities for making the best of yourself and creating a positive first impression. Today we will be examining some of the techniques that can be adopted to achieve this:

- Creating a positive first impression
  - visibly (face to face)
  - invisibly (by the written word or telephone)
- Being interviewed for a job
- Self-management
  - using time
  - building confidence

One-to-one situations are good for cutting your assertive teeth. You can try out new approaches and develop new skills in fairly safe circumstances. If you are with a trusted friend you can ask for feedback to get an idea of how you are doing. When you move into the public domain and become more visible, however, you will need to turn up the level of your assertive behaviour and move from the subtle to the bold. More of this tomorrow.

In order to create a good first impression, you will need to manage the perceptions of others. This may be accomplished through the persona you project – which may, of course, be light years from the one you revert to in private. This is fine as long as you are happy to handle the discontinuity.

Creating a positive first impression – visibly

The first opportunity we have to create a good impression is at an initial meeting or during an interview for a job.

It is undoubtedly true that human beings are incredibly judgemental. We generally look for similarities in those we are meeting for the first time because this reinforces us as individuals and gives us common ground to explore. We are less tolerant of those who take diametrically opposed views to our own or who live by a different set of values.

When meeting someone for the first time, you can be absolutely sure that they have this lightning ability, as you do of course, to sum you up in something under 10 seconds and be utterly convinced that their powers of perception are completely accurate! You have only these very few seconds, therefore, to create the impression of your choice.

Very often our first impressions are proved wrong in the long run. However, it does take an inordinate amount of time to dismantle a first impression and substitute for it a more accurate one.

Let us now examine the many factors that go in to creating a
first impression:

- Appearance
- Size, mobility and national origin
- Handshake
- Gait, body language
- Voice, accent, speech pattern, speech impediment,
  tone, etc.

Judgements will be made on a combination of some or all of
the above factors before we start saying anything of
consequence.

We will look at these factors one by one.

Appearance

In order to decide *how* to make your impact, you must first determine *what* impression you wish to create. An obvious point, perhaps, but often neglected.

Here are some factors to consider when planning your impact:

- The culture of the target organisation
- The nature of the job
- The note you wish to strike with your clothes
  - a large amount of bright *colour* can be overpowering
  - *style* can be appropriate/conventional/ unconventional
  - accessories – shoes, ties, scarves, hairstyle, hair colour, jewellery, bags, belts and briefcases all contribute to the overall impression

If you decide to create the image of a non-conformist – beware. Although this gives you greater freedom and enormous scope for painting a very individualistic picture, it is a high-risk strategy, especially in a conventional environment. The question to ask yourself is: How seriously do I want this job?

Size, mobility and national origin

There is very little most of us can do about our size, degree of mobility or origin, especially at short notice. Unfortunately, it is undeniable that these factors strongly influence a first impression, so be aware of them and quickly remove any concern that the interviewer may have.

If you think that you may encounter some form of prejudice, be proud and be direct. This is very disarming and will soon put the issue (if any) into the background, leaving you with the upper hand. It will also create a relaxed atmosphere for further discussion. This is an essential step to take if there is any possibility that the interviewer will perceive a physical barrier to your suitability for the job. Deal with likely issues honestly and without apology, then move on.

Here are some examples that illustrate how an interviewee can remove prejudice at the outset:

'Although you can see I am very large, I would like to reassure you that this does not hinder my performance.'

'I would like you to know that my physical restrictions have enabled me to develop other skills to an extremely high level.'

In America, legislation is now in place to protect individuals from the effects of prejudice on the basis of size, age and looks as well as of colour, race and creed. It is a sad indictment of human society that we have to go to these lengths to protect those that fall outside the 'norm'.

Handshake

Within the first split second of meeting someone for the first time, we are there, proffering our hand as the best etiquette has taught us.

There are many varieties of handshake, some desperately disconcerting, others, businesslike and almost unremarkable.

The conclusions we draw from a handshake are out of all proportion to its significance. However, getting it wrong puts a large obstacle in the way of creating a good impression.

We have all experienced the limp handshake . . . the 'end of fingers' handshake . . . the ferocious 'bone-breaker' . . . the sweaty handshake . . . and the 'won't let go' handshake . . .

The model way to shake someone's hand is to:

- Offer an open hand, your palm facing towards to other's palm
- Look the other party in the eye and smile (try not to be manic)
- Take a firm hold of their hand and shake it up and down once or twice (no more)
- Release (If you are going to wipe, wipe discretely)

Gait, body positioning

Body language will be dealt with in much greater detail on Friday, but as we are on the subject of first impressions, it is necessary to touch on the matter here.

How you enter a room, move towards a greeting, walk or sit all goes towards forming an early impression.

Assertive behaviour can also be demonstrated non-verbally in the following three ways:

- Moving assertively (including the handshake)
- Sitting assertively
- Use of the voice (yes, it is considered to be a non-verbal mode of communication)

Moving assertively: when preparing to enter a room, knock firmly on the door and wait for a response. Once you have been asked to 'come in', open the door fully, step in and close the door behind you. Walk confidently into the room towards the greeting, hand at the ready.

Don't be timid. If you tap lightly on the door, no one will hear and you won't be asked to 'come in'. Then you will probably be anxious and uncertain – you have sabotaged yourself.

If you creep round the door, hug the wall and shuffle hesitantly towards the greeting, you will appear insipid and lacking in confidence. This is typical passive behaviour. However, if you stride in, throw your briefcase down and sit without being invited to do so, it will not appear confident, as you hope, but aggressive.

Sitting assertively: sit straight and tend to lean slightly forward. This gives the impression of meeting someone part way on their territory and looks interested and enthusiastic.

If you slouch or lean back on your shoulder blades with your bottom pivoting precariously on the edge of the chair, you will appear uninterested and disrespectful.

Contrarily, if you sit huddled and small with your toes pointing together and your hands gripped firmly between your knees, you will look childlike and helpless.

Voice: there are many dimensions to your voice, most of which are difficult to control, such as a national or regional accent, a speech impediment or the quality of your vocal cords.

Some of the vocal properties that you can control are the clarity of your speech, the pitch, the tone and the speed of delivery.

The words that you use, the grammatical patterns you favour when constructing your sentences, and the way you reinforce what you are saying with your hands all have a direct bearing on how you will be perceived, albeit unconsciously. More of this later.

Creating a positive first impression – invisibly

Our first contact with a person may be by letter, often

accompanied by a curriculum vitae (CV), or on the telephone.

Because these modes of communication are stripped of the normally abundant visible information such as appearance, style, movement and, in the case of the written word, voice, it becomes all the more important to make the most of what is left. 'Remote' modes of communication are still filled with opportunities for creating a good first impression.

We will look at the potential of these forms of communication in turn.

Letter
There are significant advantages to making your first impression by letter. When initial contact is made through the written word, you have the luxury of time to plan the impression you wish to create.

Listed below are some useful tips on how to create a good impression by letter.

- Ensure that the quality of the paper and the appearance of the writing is excellent: no spelling mistakes, daubs of tippex, colloquialisms or bad grammar.
- Handwritten letters are fine if you possess a 'good hand' that is attractive and legible. Many bad characteristics are associated with poor handwriting. Typed or word-processed letters can look very smart these days so do use one of these methods if you can.

- Make sure that what you have to say is succinct and to the point. Any information that you give in addition to what is necessary should be carefully chosen. It will reveal what is most significant to you and say something about your priorities. At best, this could benefit you enormously, particularly if you have done your research properly.

Curriculum vitae (CV)

There are certain 'rules' you should follow when compiling your curriculum vitae, many of them echoing those listed above .

The main purpose of a CV is to set out your personal details, qualifications, background experience and achievements. Information on your hobbies and social life is embellishment and not always necessary.

As a rough guide, the CV should cover no more than two sides of A4 paper; if possible, only one. All redundant information – holiday jobs that you held as a teenager and so on – should be pruned away. The people who read CVs have a very short attention span, so make it interesting but concise.

Some people have a variety of CVs from which they choose for different purposes. Each one emphasises an aspect of their past experience that is relevant for the job in question. This helps in the pre-selection process and guides the interviewer towards appropriate questions.

A trend that seems to be gathering momentum at a frightening rate just now is the inclusion of a photograph. I do wonder if this is such a good idea when you consider the notoriety of passport photographs.

The telephone
When communicating by telephone, you have the luxury of being invisible so you can get really comfortable with yourself and what you plan to say.

Here are some helpful tips on making a good first impression using the telephone:

- Do not use a mobile
- Smile when your call is answered; this can be heard in your voice
- Use a pleasant greeting and state your name and purpose clearly
- Plan what you are going to say (writing down key words will ensure you cover all the essential points)
- If you are trying to get your thoughts together, pace about if it helps and use gestures
- If you are interrupted during your call, explain what has happened so that your failing concentration does not appear rude or uninterested
- Summarise and confirm all agreements verbally so that you can be sure you have understood accurately
- Establish who will initiate the next contact; if you are anxious, it is as well to take the responsibility for this yourself
- It is often useful to follow up a telephone conversation with a letter of confirmation

- If you seem to be listening for a long time, acknowledge what is being said by using terms like 'Ah ha', 'Mmmm' and 'Yes'. Long silences can sound as if you are no longer there or have stopped paying attention
- If you find you need to be assertive, stand up while talking on the telephone; it really does help to convey a feeling of strength

Assertive interviewing skills

Many specialists books have been written on the subject of 'the interview'. However, this section would not be complete without some reference to listening skills, open questions and responding appropriately to questions – all of which are vital tools to wield when being interviewed. On

Friday we will explore the use of body language to develop rapport.

During a professionally conducted interview, the interviewer should talk for 5–10 per cent of the time only. Ideally, therefore, you will have the remainder of the time to give as much relevant information about yourself as possible.

Your curriculum vitae will have conveyed all the professional, technical and experiential information necessary to determine your suitability for the post. The interview is primarily geared towards finding out whether you will fit in to the culture of the organisation and work effectively with the rest of the team.

You will be prompted to give information about yourself through 'open questions'.

Listen out for these because they provide you with the opportunity to show yourself in a good light. They will come in the form:

- 'What made you decide to . . . ?'
- 'How would you tackle . . . ?'
- 'Explain more about how you . . . ' and so on.

They are 'open' because you determine the content and limits of the answer; there are no bounds to them. They give you masses of scope to talk about your approach and your achievements. 'Closed' questions, for comparison, are such as:

- 'How long did you work for . . . ?'
- 'How many staff were you responsible for at . . . ?'
- 'When did you pass your driving test?'

These questions prompt short, defined responses and, as a consequence, the interviewer has to work extremely hard to extract sufficient information from you to reach a decision.

If you happen to be at an interview where the interviewer asks you 'closed' questions, take the initiative and open them up yourself, saying something like:

- 'Yes, I enjoyed being an apprentice *because* it gave me an opportunity to . . .'
- 'I worked for 'Hobson's Choice' for ten years and thoroughly enjoyed it *because* it developed my ability to . . .'

Remember, undertake some basic research on the organisation and the nature of its business before you attend an interview. Interviewers often ask 'What do you know about this organisation?' You can impress easily with a knowledgeable response to this question.

Self-management

Using time
It has long been claimed that time marches on inevitably – relentlessly, even – in small, measured steps. Time is based on the natural frequency of the element, caesium. Indeed,

there is a caesium clock in Paris that acts as a time reference-point for the entire world. Time? We are obsessed with it.

It is a bold step, you may think, to step outside the belief system harboured by many eminent scientists and dispute the properties of this phenomenon called 'time', but step outside it we shall. We will learn to bend it, move it, expand and contract it – all in the presence of clear, heart-felt objectives.

Surely, we must all share the experience of having had a million and one things to do, believing that it was not humanly possible to complete them, yet found that we were sitting down at the end of the day with everything done and time enough for a relaxed cup of tea.

The secret of expanding time is having:

- *Vision* – a clear understanding of what needs to be done
- *A plan* – a prioritised list of tasks to execute
- *Method* – a knowledge of how to execute the tasks
- *Impetus* – a determination or motivation to accomplish everything on the list

You will be able to identify this framework in the high achievers in your organisation. Why not adopt it for yourself?

Look out for time warps too. They usually happen when we are in the midst of a pleasant experience, like a holiday. At the time it feels endless; but when you return home, it feels as if it happened in a different lifetime. It's rather like watching a balloon drifting towards you: as it approaches, it looks as if it is travelling really slowly; however, when it moves on past you, it takes on the properties of a meteor and disappears at the speed of light.

We can either court this phenomenon or reject it.

To court it, extract the most pleasure out of every moment and/or completely absorb yourself in the task.

To reject it, keep returning to the problems.

As managers, or in our personal lives, the truth is that when we are focused, determined and clear, time will allow us the space we need to achieve all that we wish. Give no room to negativity or doubt and you can be sure that the time will be there.

The opposite is also true, of course. When you are bored, dissipated and uninspired, an hour can feel like aeons.

Phrases like 'Well, you'll just have to make time!' are based on truth, however much we may resent it. Busy people make time all the time.

*Time is only a question of perception – we must unlearn our
conditioning, it is limiting us.*

Building confidence

To close the learning for today, let us look at what creating a
positive image is all about – *confidence*.

By adopting some of the techniques and attitudes given to
you today, you will soon begin to trust that you are capable
of forming and maintaining an image that pleases you.
Initially, one small success is all you can ask for yourself.
Having this safely behind you will be the beginning of
building confidence. Start with something you find
relatively easy, and move on to greater things from there.

Good habits, firmly established, are soon drawn into the
subconscious. When you have progressed this far, you will
find that your confidence level has increased significantly.
Confidence and a healthy self-esteem are priceless assets
and, if you are not fortunate enough to possess them
naturally, they are well worth working for.

A positive mental attitude is key. Many managers have
learned this from the experience of athletes who develop
their minds as well as their bodies. Belief in yourself,
coupled with professional expertise, will ensure your
success.

Being assertive in the public arena

Yesterday we looked at ways of creating a positive impression in one-to-one situations: at a job interview, on the telephone and through the written word.

Today we are going to look at how to develop this transient first impression into a durable professional image. To this end, we will concentrate on your ability to communicate assertively in public, among work colleagues and customers. As you grow in professional stature, you will increasingly find yourself in situations where many pairs of eyes will be watching you. You will be visible to a wider public.

Much of the assertive behaviour about to be described will be applicable to more than one arena. Here we will focus on four of the most frequently met situations in which your ability to communicate assertively will reap great rewards:

- Meetings
- Negotiations
- Presentations
- 'On-the-spot' interviews

Meetings

Meetings are often dominated by the most aggressive members of the group. In these circumstances, passive attendees can feel completely overtaken by events because they feel unable to interject and make their points. Passive types will often revert to passive/aggressive behaviour on such occasions – deafeningly 'loud' body language and more than a few sighs – or they will become silent and resign themselves to the decisions made without their input.

A good chairperson will ensure that the meeting is properly orchestrated and that everyone is given the opportunity to contribute. Often this leadership is sadly lacking, however, and meetings either take on the air of a battlefield or wander off the point and waste a lot of time – a common complaint.

For the purposes of illustrating how to handle meetings assertively, we will look at the worst scenario: that of a disorganised gathering dominated by one or two aggressive types. We will pepper this image with a few passive and passive/aggressive characters who are nursing 'hidden agendas'.

After a few words on how to prepare for a meeting, we will pull the above scenario apart and look at each component individually.

- Assertive vs aggressive
- Assertive vs passive/aggressive
- Assertive vs passive
- Assertive vs hidden agenda

Preparing for a meeting
Before attending a meeting, make sure that you have a copy of the agenda and that you fully understand why the meeting has been called.

Take with you all the supporting information you are likely to need. If you are not clear why a particular item has been included on the agenda, ask beforehand.

Make sure you know where the meeting is being held and get there on time. You will lose credibility if you turn up late, confused or ill-prepared and it will then be much harder to make an assertive and constructive contribution.

Assertive vs aggressive

Let's start by dealing with the aggressive component of the meeting.

Aggressive behaviour often works in the short term. It intimidates and controls those who fear it, and many do. However, it is not worth adopting aggressive behaviour as a long-term strategy. Eventually colleagues will get angry. The demonstrable lack of regard and respect that the aggressive person exhibits will eventually lead to uncooperative and undermining responses. Once commitment has been lost, there is no way forward for the aggressor.

The use of assertive behaviour in these circumstances can, however, draw the aggressor towards a healthier realm of communication. Here's how.

When faced with aggressive behaviour, be calm, breathe deeply and know that others at the meeting will be gunning for you. One word of caution, however: assertive behaviour is about taking responsibility for yourself, not for others; so don't speak for the group, speak for yourself. Use 'I' language.

You may have to field anger, criticism and insults before you can start taking control of the communication. Remember though, aggressive behaviour is weak behaviour. Be confident; you *can* handle it.

Here is a checklist for dealing with aggressive behaviour:

- Be calm; listen carefully
- Take a deep breath and look for an opportunity to speak. If you need to interrupt, try to catch the speaker's eye and indicate your wish to contribute. If the speaker is hell-bent on avoiding eye contact, call their name politely and state your intention to contribute
- Match the volume of your interruption to the volume of the speaker's voice
- Once you have successfully entered the dialogue, acknowledge what has just been said, then lead off with an 'I' statement. For instance: 'I understand the point you are making, but I feel we could achieve more by . . . '
- If you are dismissed, repeat your comment in a different way. Repeat yourself assertively until you have been heard

- Once you have the floor you may find you need to halt a 'return play' interruption. In this case, raise your hand to signal 'stop'. Using the person's name increases the power of your gesture
- Summarise and confirm your understanding of a point or agreement before moving on
- If you have not succeeded in making your point, register the fact. For example: 'I know that you are keen to cover a lot of ground in this meeting, but I still feel . . . '
- Maintain dignity even if you are frustrated and reassert yourself on a later occasion. Persistence really does win out in the end and you will become more effective each time you attempt assertive behaviour

Assertive vs passive/aggressive

Passive/aggressive behaviour is 'reluctant victim' behaviour. It attempts to be manipulative. A person may be angry with themselves for giving away their power, so they do it with a bad grace. This type of behaviour causes bad atmospheres, resentment, embarrassment and confusion. Often, one thing is said but the message is completely different. For instance:

Manager: 'Our best customer has just placed an urgent order, would you mind processing it immediately?'

Sales Assistant (sarcastically): 'No, that's fine, I have all the time in the world!'

Passive/aggressive behaviour is thinly disguised. In a meeting setting it may exhibit itself through overt body language – rolling the eyes heavenward, exaggerated shifting in the chair, or impatient tapping with a pen.

Here are some ideas for dealing with passive/aggressive behaviour:

- Expose the 'hidden' message, whether verbal or non-verbal. For example: 'I see that you are feeling negatively about this, would you mind discussing your objection openly?'
- Ask for their thoughts on the topic of obvious dispute
- Listen actively and respond

The passive/aggressive person has several options when their behaviour is exposed. They can rise to the challenge and redeem themselves; deny sending the message in the first place claiming that you are paranoid; or get defensive. The first option is obviously the best strategy; the latter two will without fail diminish their standing in others' eyes.

Assertive vs passive
Passive behaviour attempts to engender feelings of sympathy in others. It is as manipulative as passive/ aggressive behaviour but it pretends to be virtuous. Martyrs are classic passive types; all very laudable, but rather unpalatable. Passive people have very little self-respect, they do not stand up for themselves and tend to get 'put upon' because they are frightened to say 'no' and be rejected.

A distinguishing characteristic of a passive person is the use of silence. This can sometimes go on for a very long time and usually covers up running dialogue in their mind which is 'victim' based ('Why are you picking on me?' 'I wish you would shut up and leave me out of this!').

Dealing with a passive person is not dissimilar to handling the passive/aggressive approach. First, expose their abdication:

'I am not clear where you stand on this issue, would you tell me what your feelings are?' (Note the use of the 'I' statement and the 'open' question, 'what?')

Match silence with silence. It takes an *extremely* passive person to remain mute in the teeth of a silent and expectant gaze, especially if everyone at the meeting is engaged in the same tactic. Once they start to talk, use your active listening skills to encourage the flow.

However, if you lose patience with their silence, repeat your comment or try a different approach if you think this will help. If you get to a point of exasperation, inform the passive person that you will have to deduce their feelings if they are not prepared to share them and that you will have to proceed according to your deductions. Invite them to support you in your course of action.

Assertive vs hidden agenda

You will inevitably come across people who play their cards very close to their chest, especially in organisations where internal politics are prominent. In these cultures, people are always on the defensive, protecting themselves from exploitation or disadvantage. Sometimes this fear is imaginary, sometimes it is real, but whatever the cause, you will need common techniques to deal with it.

You will probably be able to identify the 'political animals' among your colleagues because their behaviour will appear inconsistent. They will apparently change their opinion or approach without reason, leaving a trail of confusion and uncertainty behind them. Once this erratic style has caught your attention, look at the interplay of circumstances and try to identify the likely political, and usually personal, gain that is being sought. You may then be close to the real motivation of that person.

Significant coincidences that benefit one individual do not usually occur without some help. Look for coincidences, therefore, and identify the beneficiaries. Coupled with hindsight, the hidden agenda may suddenly be revealed to you and past, previously confusing, behaviours will fall into context. This knowledge is useful; it is power. Do not try to tackle the individual. Hidden agendas, by their very nature, can always be denied and you will end up looking paranoid or foolish.

It is probably worth testing your theory by predicting the likely reaction of your colleague in certain circumstances. If, when these circumstances occur, your prediction proves correct, the hidden agenda is likely to be what you suspected. If not, think again; maybe you *are* paranoid!

Having understood a colleague's private motivation, you will have a clear picture of where you fit into the pattern of things. This will enable you to plan your own approach. This could be one of avoidance, of course, if you choose not to get caught up in the politics of the organisation; or it may be a strategic option – the choice as always, is yours.

Here is a checklist for identifying a hidden agenda:

- Examine coincidences that benefit one person, or a specific group of people
- Look out for inconsistent behaviour: this may take the form of an unlikely relationship, non-verbal messages or a sudden and inexplicable abdication of responsibility
- Put your observations into context using hindsight; this may help you identify the 'hidden agenda' specifically
- Test your theory as innocuously and as anonymously as possible
- It is probably best to keep your own counsel, you may be able to do more to advantage yourself in this way

- If you are going to tackle someone on their private agenda, be absolutely sure of your ground and that you can handle it in the most assertive way possible. Some tips on this were given in the passages dealing with passive/aggressive or purely passive behaviour
- Look for a motivation: if you are suddenly flavour of the month with someone who is known to be ambitious, ask yourself why
- Be vigilant: it would be naïve to think that hidden agendas are not being worked out somewhere within your organisation

Negotiations

There are some very simple rules for conducting yourself effectively – and assertively – in negotiations.

Negotiations can fall into several categories. First, there are those taking place in the working environment with one other person such as your boss, a colleague or a member of your staff. Moving up in scale, the meeting room often witnesses negotiations among several colleagues whose views reside in different camps. Then there are those conducted between two opposing parties. When these two parties cannot agree, they may resort to the services of an arbitrator or mediator.

Whatever the situation, whether it is simple problem-solving or a full-scale meeting between managers and a trade union, the basic rules for successful negotiating are the same. More often than not, it is merely a question of scale.

Here are the basic steps for negotiating successfully:

- Know exactly what you wish to achieve and be absolutely clear on the level of your authority
- Be assertive and use positive body language
- Make sure you understand the other's viewpoint
- Convey your own viewpoint clearly and state your desired outcome
- Look for areas of common ground to reinforce mutual interests and to develop a commitment to a satisfactory resolution
- Listen actively and demonstrate understanding throughout the discussion

- Never bluff, fudge, manipulate or lie
- Never offer something you cannot deliver
- If you are feeling pressured, ask for a recess
- Communicate your proposals clearly and concisely and establish those of the other party
- Summarise the areas of difference and explore the extent of these; identify the issues where compromise is possible
- Having distilled out the main area of contention, discuss any concessions that you are both prepared to make
- Summarise, agree and confirm in writing

Presentations

Presentations strike fear into the hearts of most managers, whatever their seniority. They are one of the most visible and exposed professional platforms and can leave your image enhanced, intact or in tatters.

Usually you will have advance warning of the requirement to make a presentation and will also, therefore, have time to prepare and practise for the occasion.

These two points are most important: *prepare* and *practise*.

Those who are 'naturals' at making presentations are the exception rather than the rule. Most good presenters are only good because they have invested time in preparation and practice. Everyone can do it if they try – and everyone *can* enjoy the experience.

There is nothing more satisfying than the flow of success when you step down from the platform having made an excellent presentation. It really is worth investing the time and energy to get it right.

Of course, much has been written on presentation skills, and clearly justice cannot be done to the subject in a few short paragraphs. However, here are a few pointers to help you add this mode of communication to the assertiveness toolkit you are assembling.

Preparation and practice

- Make sure you understand the purpose of the presentation
- Have a clear impression of your audience, their level and their expectations; this will enable you to pitch your presentation correctly
- Prepare your talk:
  Beginning – Tell them what you are going to say
  Middle – Say it
  End – Tell them what you have said
  (Most people will only retain about three points)
- Prepare visual aids:
  Overhead projector slides – These should *add* to your presentation; they should be bold, clear and *never* more than a paragraph
  Handouts – These can contain more detailed information along with copies of your overhead slides. They should be of top quality
  35mm slides – Not always an advantage as you have to make your presentation in a darkened room. Not everyone can handle technology competently, either. If you do use them, they should be clear and concise
- Prepare a set of cards with keyword prompts, facts or difficult names on them to help you while you are nervous
- Practise – in front of a mirror, colleagues, friends and family. Make sure you get the timing right and get your audience to fire awkward questions at you

Making the presentation

- Wear clean, comfortable and conservative clothes. If you don't, your audience will pay more attention to your attire than to what you have to say
- Arrive in plenty of time; familiarise yourself with the equipment and check your slides are in the right order
- Make sure you have a glass of water handy in case your mouth dries up
- If you are using torch pointers, telescopic pointers or infra-red remote controls – practise (watch out for shake)
- Relax, by whatever means suits you
- Tell your audience what you expect from them in terms of interruptions, discussion or questions; you may prefer to take these as you go along, or leave them to the end
- Enjoy your talk but remain vigilant: it is too easy to be drawn into letting your guard down and saying something contentious. If you cannot answer a question, be honest about it and tell the questioner that you will find out and get back to them
- Try to avoid jokes. There is usually at least one person in the audience who will take offence
- Don't talk down to your audience, but equally, don't assume they understand the technicalities of your subject
- Pause from time to time. This is a performance, and pauses are useful for dramatic effect – and to collect your thoughts
- Of course, *use assertive language and body posture*

On-the-spot interviews

Increasingly, managers are required to field questions from the media.

With the rapid growth in local television stations, radio stations and local newspapers, it may only be a matter of time before a journalist is going to ferret you out and ask you some questions about some aspect of your business. Whether you are subjected to a 'hostile' interview or a 'friendly' one, the experience can be awesome – especially if there are lights, camera crew and a floor manager present.

Commonly, now, chief executives are trying to project a more approachable image through acquainting themselves with individual members of their organisations. Increasingly, too, organisations are being encouraged to take responsibility for developing a two-way relationship with the communities in which their organisations belong. These new trends will lead towards much greater public awareness and interest in your business.

When approached by an interviewer or journalist, you may feel very exposed. However, here are some guidelines for dealing with this experience.

First, *don't panic* (this one is easy if you are now fully assertive and confident).

Second, remember, if someone is wanting information from you, *you hold the power*. Unless they are prepared to floor you, they will have to wait until you are ready to deliver.

Third, if you are unsure of what you want to say, ask for time to consider your response. If the questioner is persistent, smile, repeat your need for time, acknowledge their position and explain that you would rather they had accurate information than that which could be misleading.

Beware: if a journalist starts getting chatty with you after the interview and asks for your opinion on a contentious matter, watch out; you may think that the interview has ended, but it usually hasn't.

Taking stock of progress

By now you should have started to gather together some useful tools for developing your assertive skills. You may have had a chance to practise some of these techniques and found that they really do work. These early successes should increase your confidence and fire your enthusiasm to learn more, take control and have the courage to set your own goals.

Body language

Today, we will look at some forms of body language which have the most impact on others. This is by no means an exhaustive study of the subject, but it will maximise the effect you can create when you communicate assertively.

The following areas will comprise today's learning:

- Assertive body language
- The use of gestures
- Developing rapport
- The use of verbal language
- Interpreting body language

Your body really can speak louder than words.

Assertive body language

Because your body conveys such a large proportion of what you are communicating, it is worth concentrating on this area for a short time and considering what it is we convey with our bodies and how we can be sabotaged by them.

It is a useful exercise to 'body watch' – but try to be discreet. You will notice that when two people are engrossed in riveting conversation, they are completely unaware of their bodies. (Unless the conversation is skirting around sex of course; in these circumstances we are *very* unsubtle.) We use our bodies at the unconscious level, therefore, to emphasise points or to transmit secondary messages.

Assertive behaviour is distinguished by the continuity between the verbal and the non-verbal. In other words, your body reflects precisely what you are saying when you are in 'assertive mode'.

Try saying 'Look over there,' without using some part of your body to point. Indeed, you could draw someone's attention to something without using words at all, only gestures. This is a crude example of the power of body language, but it serves to illustrate that we are driven to use it, and, what's more, it is the dominant channel of communication.

Just think how obvious it can be when you are nervous. Your body will communicate this rather than the message you are trying to transmit verbally.

The primary vehicle for body language is emotion. Control your emotions and you will be able to control your messages. Try not to go to extremes, though.

To start being 'body aware', therefore:

- 'Body watch' (without staring too obviously)
- Ask for feedback from your colleagues and friends on your own use of body language
- Have an imaginary conversation in front of the mirror (very embarrassing at first, but you will get used to it) and see if you can identify the way you use gestures and the amount of gestures you use

Because of the restricted time and space available here for this topic, we will merely waltz through the most potent aspects of body language.

- Space
- Stance
- Touch

Space
We all carry with us an egg-shaped exclusion zone which varies in size in direct proportion to our circumstances, purpose and level of comfort. As a point of interest, you can usually measure the size of someone's 'egg' by the length of their focal attention. On a tube train, this is almost zero (people often look glazed or they focus on reading matter); at work it can extend to include one person or a small gathering of people; at a large presentation, it can reach to the extremities of an entire hall.

Mostly, varying the size of the 'egg' is an instinctive part of our behaviour. However, it can be very useful to understand the nature of 'personal space' so that it can be used to good effect.

Learning point I: *if we do not include people in our personal space, it is impossible to influence them.*

Notice how you 'shut down' when someone you dislike comes too close, or someone you're not sure about comes too close too soon. I'm sure we have all experienced backing away from someone as they repeatedly trespass on our personal territory until the next step takes us through the window or into a cupboard.

Remember, too, a time when you were part of a vast audience, and the presenter or entertainer made you feel as if you were the only person in the room. This was because they extended their personal space to include you.

Notice how you use your own space, and how you act differently with family, colleagues and those in authority. As an exercise, practise drawing your space in until its boundaries meet your body. Then try filling a room with your presence by expanding your space. You can do this by changing the point of your focal and conscious attention. Accompany this with a visualisation of yourself as either completely invisible or extraordinary influential.

Learning point II: *the more space you use, the more impact you will have.*

Naturally tall people have an advantage because, by definition, they occupy a large amount of space. Yet these people are often shy and withdrawn by nature. Perhaps they are this way because they do not have the confidence to handle their own natural authority.

Short people, on the other hand, can make up for their lack of size by adopting a good assertive style, and indeed, a large number of short people have been extraordinarily successful. Unfortunately, however, their communication style sometimes overcompensates for their lack of physical stature and becomes aggressive.

There are ways, however, of sitting and standing that look 'big' and carry huge impact. By adopting some of the following techniques, short people can actually 'grow' in others' perceptions.

Here are some techniques for creating presence:

Assertive standing: stand straight and 'think' tall. Try not to twine your legs around each other or stand with your weight upon one leg. Nothing destroys the image like crumpling onto the floor because you have overbalanced!

When you wish to communicate powerfully, again, stand straight, feet planted firmly on the floor, body centred, hands at your side. If it is hard to push you over physically, it will be hard to push you around verbally.

Assertive sitting: convey confidence by using as much space as possible while sitting. Sit with your body at an angle, well back in the chair and place your arms on the armrests. Sit 'small' and you will be perceived as small.

Stance
Your posture will convey a huge impression, so it is important to get it right.

Everyone will notice someone who stands upright and walks well. This is a good habit to cultivate. It portrays confidence and authority.

Tall people are notorious for stooping and they always say it is because they can't get through the doors. However, it is an enviable gift to be tall; many would give their eye teeth for height – so, if you are tall, duck only when necessary. Stoop when you are young and you will have no choice but to stoop when you are old.

Short people can walk tall too. In fact, people of under five foot three can look six foot tall if they stand proud. We often confuse confidence for size, so you can make the most of this misconception by cultivating your own personal stature.

Touch

Taking the liberty to touch someone conveys superiority. A boss can pat his staff on the back, but they would probably feel uncomfortable reciprocating this action. A pat on the back is an authoritative action. If it remains unchallenged, a hierarchy is established.

A good way of putting things back on an even footing is to look for an immediate opportunity to touch them back. You might say 'Excuse me' as you pick a hair off their jacket, or say 'You've brushed up against some dust' as you sweep their chest briskly with the back of your hand.

The use of gestures

Gestures can either reinforce your communication or they can draw attention away from what you are saying. They

should be used prudently, therefore, to maximise their
effect.

Gestures include everything from 'windmill' arms (sit on
your hands if this is you) to almost imperceptible
movements of the face, head, torso or arms – they rarely
involve the use of the legs.

The most common gestures are made with hands alone and
they serve to emphasise what is being said by the mouth.

The type of gesture you choose to use can indicate
something about your personality. If you 'prod the air' more
than artistically necessary, you will appear aggressive. Open
gestures, arms out away from the body, can indicate an
open and warm personality. Be too energetic and untidy
with your movements and you will come across as
shambolic and disorganised – especially if this is the style of
your dress also. No gesturing looks passive.

Assertive gestures tend towards the moderate ground.
Timing and relevance are crucial. They should flow
smoothly and mirror as closely as possible what is being
said.

Developing rapport

Empathising with another does not depend solely on the
words you use. Much of the rapport is carried in your body
language.

If you watch two people talking empathetically and
unselfconsciously, you will probably notice that their bodies
take on virtually the same demeanour. For example, both

may have crossed their legs, put an elbow on the table and their chin in the palm of their hands. If they are drinking, you will often find that the drinks diminish at exactly the same rate. They will have *matched* and *mirrored* each other's behaviour. If you do this consciously, but subtly, you will find that your ability to build rapport will have improved greatly.

Should you find yourself in an unpleasant or fraught conversation and you wish to alleviate the tension, it is possible to do this also by matching and mirroring the other's body language. Having matched and held their body position for some time, you can start moving your own body towards a more relaxed position. You will soon find that they start mirroring you and the tension will fade. It is impossible to remain aggressive when you are physically relaxed.

Beware, though: if you are not sufficiently subtle in your mirroring and matching skills, it will look as if you are mimicking the other's behaviour. If this is the impression you create, it will be very difficult to make amends.

Couple this technique with good eye contact, active listening skills, lots of head nods, 'Ah ha', 'Mmmm' and so on, and you will be able to build rapport with the best of them.

Being able to empathise with someone involves understanding their feelings by getting beneath the surface. This can often be achieved by being able to relate what they are saying to a similar experience of your own. If you are at sea however, with no common understanding, the mirroring and matching technique can be used to engender the same feelings in you that are being experienced by the other person. If the other person has lost confidence, for instance, and takes on the foetal position, try it out for yourself and see what emotions it brings up. You will probably gain a better understanding of their feelings and be able to empathise more effectively.

The use of verbal language

The words we choose and the way we construct sentences can assist us in the process of building rapport.

To illustrate this, think of the way we talk to children. We are constantly reflecting back to them the words they use themselves. It has to be said that sometimes we diminish their intellects, but nonetheless, the principle is the same. Listen out for the kind of words used by the person with whom you are trying to build rapport and reflect this style of language back to them.

A manager often uses a distinctive language that is related to the function or specialism of his or her role. Finance, information technology, manufacturing, design and development all have their own language. If you use this language back to these specialists, they will feel comfortable with your style. Use a different language, and they will feel alienated.

Here are some examples of language compatibility:

A financier's language includes words like: balance, *bottom line*, assets, investments, *credit*, etc.

Some of the following words would be used by an information technologist: *logical*, *image*, capacity, network, hardware, *upgrade*, etc.

The same sentence can be constructed differently for each audience.

To the financier: 'On *balance*, I feel it would be to our *credit* . . .'

To the information technologist: 'It would seem the most *logical* approach to *upgrade* our *image* by . . .'

And to a visionary designer whose language may include words like: *see*, impact, style, colour, *create*, proportion, *impression* etc: 'I can *see* that we could *create* the best *impression* by . . .'

Interpreting body language

BEWARE: this is not an exact science.

When watching someone for the tell-tale signs of a hidden

message, don't only engage your brain, engage your senses too. People often *think* that they are privy to the inner secrets of another person, but you have to be bordering on the telepathic really to *know*.

However, here are a few guidelines to interpreting body language.

Be aware of the environment in which you are making your observation. If it is cold, your subject may have a tense jaw or their arms may be folded tightly across their bodies. In these circumstances, they *may not* be either nervous or aggressive – but then again, *they may*.

Watch for 'leakage'. Leakage happens to someone who, say, is controlling their nerves, to all intents and purposes, extremely well. However, nerves have to exhaust themselves somewhere so watch for toes curling and uncurling at the end of shoes; muscles clenching and unclenching round the jaw, grinding teeth, rattling change in the pocket and quivering knees. As resourceful human beings, we have many such outlets.

Mostly look for discontinuity and coincidence.

If someone is pledging their unequivocal support but shaking their head as they do so – watch your back.

If someone says 'I never lie' at the same time as moving their pointing finger from side to side – don't believe them. This is the gesture of denial – their body is denying the statement.

If someone says, 'I am not interested in scoring points with the boss' and yet is coincidentally around the boss at the most politically charged moments, watch you don't get sideswiped.

Watch people's eyes. It sounds obvious to say that people look where their interest lies, but sometimes, during an unguarded moment, it is interesting to note exactly where this is – or who it is.

Sometimes it is easier to identify 'anti' body language. People tend to be very clear when they dislike someone. You can see it in their eyes and in the way they orientate their bodies away from the object of their distaste. This is the opposite of mirroring. Sometimes their complete and habitual removal from the scene gives the game away.

When people like each other, they get into close proximity – into personal comfort zones. They may touch, they often have good and prolonged eye contact, they smile, reinforce and reflect each other's behaviour. Sometimes you are aware of 'chemistry', when there are no identifiable body signals. It is interesting to observe this behaviour and speculate on what it is that causes this effect.

Summary

Today, we have skated across the top of a very powerful aid to communication. We have learned that the body will not lie for you. This makes your motivation visible, much more visible than you probably realise. However, you may now be more aware and may be able to body watch from a more informed position.

We have covered:

* How your body can help you be more assertive
* How to use gesture
* How to develop rapport using mirroring and matching
* The use of language
* Developing a feel for the 'hidden message'

Remember, your body (including voice – not words) and eyes carry about 90 per cent of any message you are trying to convey. Because the proportion is so large, this aspect of communication has powerful potential. If you use your non-verbal knowledge skilfully, you will find that your level of control increases significantly.

Enjoy it.

Personal power

We have almost come full circle now, so to close this week's learning, we will discuss personal power – how to win it, how to hold it and how to succeed with it.

The interesting thing about personal power is that you don't have to be born particularly advantaged to have it. It is not *dependent* upon your looks, size, intelligence, wealth or talents. Some of these may help; but *anyone* can acquire power, be it political, professional, personal or all three.

Most, or all, of the following qualities are consistently found in powerful people:

- Clarity of vision
- Well-defined values and beliefs
- Confidence
- Powerful communication
- An ability to build relationships
- Political skill

Power remains only with those who respect it – abuse it at your peril. There may be a short-term gain for those who win power through confidence tricks, but it is inevitable that the fall from power will be in direct proportion to the 'con'.

Let's take each element of personal power and examine it separately.

Clarity of vision

It is essential to create a framework upon which you can hang your power. It is only when you know where you are going and are 100 per cent committed to getting there that you can plan the way forward to your success. It doesn't matter which path you take, or whether you change the route from time to time, as long as you keep your eye on the goal.

Identifying the goal in the first place does require vision. Once you have this, and this is usually acquired through self-knowledge, the rest will fall into place.

If you have difficulty establishing your primary goal, start with a series of smaller ones. These will soon form a pattern that will lead you towards an understanding of what you wish to achieve. Ask yourself where you would like to be in

10, 20 or 50 years' time. Is maintaining your present course and direction sufficient to give you long-term satisfaction? Don't be concerned if your goal is extraordinarily ambitious. All those who have succeeded started out with 'impossible dreams'. Equally, don't be ashamed if your goal is not particularly ambitious. This means that you are meeting your own needs extremely well and puts you way ahead of the game.

Visionaries take the following steps to create a framework upon which they can build their successes.

They:

- Identify personal goals
- See their goals clearly and imagine what it is like to have reached them
- Make a commitment to achieve them by a certain time
- Act as if their goals have already been achieved

If you don't put a time limit on the attainment of your goals, your mind will always think of them as being in the future. Acting as if you have already reached your goals will help to bring them into the present.

Test out these steps for yourself. Start small to gain confidence in the process.

Well-defined values and beliefs

Know what you value and believe. This is really much more difficult than it appears because values and beliefs have a habit of changing to suit different circumstances. Dig deep though; these underpin all your behaviours.

In the process of getting to know your values and beliefs you will have to ask yourself certain questions like: What price are you prepared to pay for your success?

- *Personally* – intimate relationships (partner, family, friends)
- *Spiritually* – what you feel is right or wrong; what you need to do to feel good about yourself

- *Professionally* – career progression, promotion
- *Politically* – being in the right place at the right time

If you ask a powerful person the question 'What price are you prepared to pay for your success?', they will have a clear, well-thought-out answer that is right for them. They are absolutely comfortable living within the framework of their values and beliefs. Any conflict – and conflict will develop from time to time as the balance of their life changes – will be addressed in the light of this value set.

Powerful people are comfortable with themselves. It is almost tangible.

Confidence

Here, we get back to the basics of *successful assertiveness*. Respect and honour yourself. You are as worthy as the next person.

Self-worth is the precursor to building confidence. If you believe in yourself, others will too.

True confidence enables you to handle any situation with aplomb. Even in situations that you have not met before, you will be able to draw on your experience and extrapolate from your past behaviour to meet the needs of the moment.

A sudden lack of confidence petrifies and paralyses the mind; all coping mechanisms seem to miraculously disappear. This rapid evacuation of all that you have learned will undermine your attempts at building confidence and put you back to square one again. So be kind to yourself; know that these things happen to everybody and that you are still a worthy individual. Forgive what you perceive to be your mistakes and move on.

The more you practise assertive behaviour, the less often sudden losses in confidence will happen. As with your goals (gaining confidence may be one of them, of course) try believing that you have already succeeded and act that way. It will soon become a reality.

Powerful communication

Powerful people are often extremely good communicators. Their communication skills are characterised by typical assertive behaviour, and more.

Having a vision is not enough. The only way a vision becomes a reality is through motivating others to play their part, and the only way to motivate is to communicate. Only in very rare cases are visions actualised in a vacuum; usually they are dependent upon someone, or many people, cooperating in some way.

Not many of us are natural orators but we can learn from those who are. Here are a few qualities that you can learn to develop in yourself.

- Vision (remember Martin Luther King – 'I have a dream . . .')
- Belief – in your purpose, your own ability and the ability of your team

- Acute observation (listening, watching, sensing)
- Ability to develop empathy
- Ability to judge the mood of the moment and respond appropriately (flexibility/intuition)
- A sense of timing and theatre

Powerful communicators regard their public appearances as theatrical performances. They create an impact, build tension, move their audience and leave them on a high.

An ability to build relationships

It is extremely difficult to build and maintain relationships at the best of times, but it is especially difficult when driven by the work environment. Nonetheless, this ability is crucial if you wish to rise to the top.

There is no magic formula for developing good relationships and they can be stamped with a variety of styles – friendly, nurturing, respectful, mysterious, controlling, aggressive and so on. Try to identify your own style and check out the impression you create with colleagues.

Professional relationships are often fraught with difficulty because they have to be developed with people who are imposed upon us, not chosen by us. Indeed, some of our colleagues we might actively avoid when out of the work environment. Building good relationships therefore demands patience, determination and the ability to step back and see things from a different perspective.

Most people do not try to be bad or difficult. If this is the behaviour that they exhibit, it usually indicates that they hold a belief that is causing them distress. If you encounter this behaviour as a manager, you may need to spend some time delving below the surface to weed out the problem. Beware, however; you cannot merely go through the motions, and you may learn some unpalatable truths about yourself in the process.

Much can be done to maintain relationships remotely (by telephone, letter, memo, etc.) but first you have to know and understand the people who work around you. This is usually done at times when the pressure is off or at times when the office socialises together. There is a fine line to tread between being too involved and too remote. You will have to determine the best balance for yourself; but remember that power-holders are often characterised by a certain amount of mystique.

A sobering thought to leave you with: people always remember your worst behaviour and this dominates their impression of you. Bear this in mind when you feel yourself about to lose your temper.

Political skill

Office politics is a minefield because the players are all working out their own personal agendas. It is an intensely self-interested activity and difficult to identify because the motivation behind the actions of others is often unknown, and conclusions about them are frequently pure speculation.

A good politician, however, can identify the game, the players and the rules through careful observation. Some, but not many, are lucky enough to be instinctive in this arena. Derived theories can be tested by injecting 'dye' to see where it reappears or by 'bait' to see who bites. This can be an extremely illuminating activity and sometimes the outcome is very surprising. Be warned, though; it can also be a dangerous game, as there are always more experienced players on the field.

Politics can be played up and down the organisation and the position that you occupy on the hierarchy or your political dexterity will determine your potential.

Controlling the way you are perceived by your colleagues is a fairly low-key 'political' activity and you owe it to yourself to do this effectively – whatever your ambitions.

Learn what you can about the interests, circumstances and ambitions of others within your organisation and identify critical relationships. Keep an eye out for those with influence and promote yourself among these people.

You may have a role model or mentor in your organisation whom you can study or learn from. Virtually all successful people can identify a person who influenced them strongly in this way and at whose feet they lay their success. Try to identify one for yourself.

Whatever you do, do it with comfort, courage and conviction. The maverick approach may sound attractive but it is an extremely risky strategy.

Summary

Today we have briefly touched upon the dominant features of *personal power*. The subject holds books' worth of potential and is a fascinating subject of study; but there is no room here to go into more detail. However, much can be understood and achieved by thinking through the points noted above and testing them out in your own professional environment.

Having picked your way through the week's lessons, you should now have the basic tools to move forward as a successful and assertive professional.

Remember, successful assertiveness ultimately boils down to three main points:

- *Understand yourself* (values, beliefs, the whys and wherefores of your nature)
- *Know yourself* (wants, predispositions, ambitions, desires)
- *Value yourself* (confidence, rights)

From this position of knowledge, you will be well placed to make your own choices – about how you wish to be perceived, how to plan your career and how to create and manage your impression.

The path to becoming truly and effectively assertive is a rewarding one. Nothing is wasted and each small step builds towards greater and greater success. Don't give up, and don't lose sight of the fact that above all else, you are entitled to this amount of control over your life.

Good luck and enjoy being assertive.

The Successful Business in a Week series

Successful Appraisals in a Week
Successful Assertiveness in a Week
Successful Budgeting in a Week
Successful Business Writing in a Week
Successful Career Planning in a Week
Finance for Non-Financial Managers in a Week
Successful Interviewing in a Week
Understanding Just in Time in a Week
Successful Leadership in a Week
Successful Marketing in a Week
Successful Market Research in a Week
Successful Meetings in a Week
Successful Motivation in a Week
Successful Presentation in a Week
Successful Project Management in a Week
Successful Public Relations in a Week
Successful Negotiating in a Week
Successful Selling in a Week
Successful Stress Management in a Week
Successful Time Managment in a Week
Understanding Total Quality Management in a Week
Doing Business in Europe